RISING ABOVE AND RISING WITH GRACE

A WOMAN'S ROADMAP TO CAREER MASTERY

DR. MINAKSHI BANSAL

Made with ♥ on the Notion Press Platform
www.notionpress.com

DEDICATION

*To the women who came before me, paving the way
with resilience and grace, and to the women who
will come after, may this book illuminate your path
to career mastery.*

ᗏᗏᗏ

Contents

Contents

Prayer

"Om Bhadram Karnebhih Shrinuyama Devah

Bhadram Pashyemakshabhiryajatrah

Sthirairangais Tushtuvamsastanubhih

Vyashema Devahitam Yadayuh

Svasti Na Indro Vriddhashravah

Svasti Nah Pusha Vishwavedah

Svasti Nastarkshyo Arishtanemih

Svasti No Brihaspatir Dadhatu

Om Shantih Shantih Shantih"

This mantra is a prayer for universal well-being, invoking the blessings of various deities for protection, health, and happiness. It emphasizes the importance of experiencing the auspicious through all senses and living a life aligned with divine purpose. The repetition of "Shantih" at the end signifies a deep desire for peace in the individual, the environment, and the universe at large. This mantra is often recited as a prayer for peace, prosperity, and the physical and spiritual well-being of all beings.

❧❧❧

About The Author

This book represents the culmination of extensive research and meticulous analysis, incorporating a diverse range of sources, including numerous books, scholarly studies, and personal experiences. Additionally, I have scoured various websites to gather relevant information and data essential for the compilation of this work. I have taken every precaution to ensure the accuracy of the information presented and have diligently cited all sources to acknowledge their contributions.

From her earliest days, Minakshi was distinguished by an insatiable appetite for reading. Her literary universe was inhabited by characters and narratives that spanned ethical tales, motivational and inspirational stories, and the mythic parables imbued with life lessons. This voracious reading habit was not merely for personal edification but was driven by a desire to distill and disseminate the essence of these narratives to foster the development of students and peers alike. She was particularly captivated by the lives and teachings of historical figures and spiritual leaders such as Adi Shankaracharya, Swami Vivekananda, Dr. APJ Abdul Kalam, Mahamana Pandit Madan Mohan Malviya, Mahatma Gandhi, Sardar Vallabhai Patel, and Vinoba Bhave, among others. Their philosophies and life stories fueled her ambition to embody their ideals of resilience, selflessness, and relentless pursuit of knowledge.

Dr. Minakshi's academic and practical engagement with psychology has been equally noteworthy. As a research scholar, her focus has been on exploring the intricate tapestry of the human psyche, aiming to unlock the potential for psychological well-being and societal harmony. Her scholarly work is complemented by her active involvement in social work, where she employs her academic insights to make tangible differences in the lives of the underprivileged. Her endeavours in social work are characterized by an innovative approach that combines traditional wisdom with contemporary psychological practices to address the multifaceted challenges faced by these communities.

Her artistic talents, another facet of her diverse capabilities, are not merely a personal passion but also serve as a medium through which she communicates and connects with others. Her art, rich in symbolism and emotional depth, reflects her philosophical inquiries and social concerns, offering viewers a glimpse into the breadth of her intellect and the depth of her compassion.

In addition to her contributions to the arts and social sciences, Dr. Minakshi has embraced the healing arts of Pranic Healing, mastering the techniques developed by Master Choa Kok Sui. This practice, which focuses on the manipulation of Prana or life energy to heal the body and aura, has been both a personal journey of discovery and a means through which she extends her healing touch to others. Her proficiency in Pranic Healing is complemented by her advocacy and teaching of various forms of meditation aimed at rejuvenation, personal betterment, and the cultivation of harmony within individuals and communities alike.

Dr. Minakshi's life is a narrative of relentless pursuit, not just of personal achievement but of the upliftment and empowerment of society at large. Her diverse interests and talents—spanning the arts, literature, psychology, and the healing practices—converge on a singular path of service. She embodies the spirit of the luminaries who inspired her, channelling their legacy through her actions and teachings. Through her books, art, and social initiatives, she continues to inspire a new generation to embark on their own journeys of self-discovery, resilience, and altruism.

Her commitment to social betterment, particularly her focus on uplifting underprivileged children, reflects a deep understanding of the transformative potential of education and personal development. By integrating her knowledge of psychology, her artistic sensibilities, and her healing practices, Dr. Bansal has developed a holistic approach to social work that addresses both the immediate needs and the long-term well-being of the communities she serves.

As an author, Dr. Minakshi's writings offer a blend of inspirational insights, practical wisdom, and reflective contemplations drawn from her extensive reading and life experiences. Her books serve as a guide for those seeking to navigate the complexities of life with grace, resilience, and purpose. Through her narratives, she extends an invitation to her readers to explore the depths of their own potential and to contribute meaningfully to the collective well-being of society.

In Dr. Minakshi Bansal, we find a remarkable synthesis of the artist, the scholar, the healer, and the social activist. Her life's work stands as a beacon of hope and a source of inspiration for individuals seeking to make a difference in the world. Her story is a compelling reminder of the power of individual action, rooted in compassion and driven by a profound commitment to the betterment of humanity. Dr. Minakshi's legacy is not just in the tangible outcomes of her efforts but in the enduring spirit of inquiry, empathy, and service that she embodies.

ନ୍ତ୍ରନ୍ତ୍ରନ୍ତ୍ର

Preface

In the tapestry of life, a woman's journey towards career mastery is a unique and intricate weave. It is a path paved with ambition, resilience, challenges, and triumphs. As I embarked on my own professional journey, I often found myself yearning for a roadmap, a guide that could navigate me through the labyrinth of workplace dynamics, personal growth, and the pursuit of fulfilling ambitions. It was this yearning that sparked the creation of this book.

This is not just a guide for climbing the corporate ladder; it is a testament to the strength, resilience, and grace that women embody in their professional lives. It's a celebration of the unique challenges we face and the innovative solutions we bring to the table.

It's an acknowledgment of the delicate balance we strive to achieve between our personal lives and our careers, and a testament to our unwavering determination to rise above and rise with grace.

Throughout these pages, you'll find insights, strategies, and stories that I hope will inspire and empower you on your own career journey. We'll delve into the importance of unleashing your inner potential, recognizing and celebrating your unique strengths and talents.

We'll explore the power of building confidence from within, challenging self-doubt, and embracing your authentic self.

We'll navigate the intricacies of workplace dynamics, from mastering the art of networking to communicating with impact and influence. We'll discuss the importance of setting powerful career goals, embracing failure as a stepping stone, and cultivating resilience and adaptability in the face of change.

We'll also delve into the transformative power of mentorship and sponsorship, advocating for diversity and inclusion, and thriving in an ever-evolving work landscape.

As women, we often face unique challenges in the workplace, from the gender pay gap to unconscious bias. This book acknowledges these challenges and provides practical strategies for overcoming them. It's about empowering you to negotiate for your worth, overcome imposter syndrome, and shatter glass ceilings.

This is a roadmap for women at all stages of their careers, from those just starting out to seasoned professionals seeking to make a greater impact.

It's a guide for women who aspire to leadership positions, those who want to create a more fulfilling work-life balance, and those who simply want to find more joy and meaning in their work.

This is more than just a book; it's a conversation, a community, a movement. It's an invitation to join a global network of women who are supporting, inspiring, and empowering each other to achieve their dreams.

I encourage you to share your stories, connect with other women in your field, and build a community of support that will lift you up and propel you forward.

In writing this book, I've drawn on my own experiences, the wisdom of mentors and colleagues, and the countless stories of women who have overcome challenges and achieved remarkable success. I hope that these pages will serve as a source of inspiration, guidance, and support as you navigate your own career journey.

Remember, the path to career mastery is not always easy. There will be setbacks, challenges, and moments of self-doubt. But with resilience, determination, and a supportive community by your side, you can overcome any obstacle and achieve your full potential.

So, embrace the journey, celebrate your successes, learn from your failures, and never stop striving for excellence. The world needs your unique talents and perspectives, and it's time for you to rise above and rise with grace.

Dr. Minakshi Bansal
Social Activist
Ahmedabad, Gujarat, Bharat

ONE

UNLEASHING YOUR INNER POTENTIAL

The journey toward career mastery begins with a profound exploration of self – a recognition of the dormant potential that resides within each woman. Unleashing this inner potential is not about becoming someone you are not, but rather, uncovering and nurturing the authentic self that is capable of extraordinary things.

This process of self-discovery starts with introspection. Take time to reflect on your values, passions, and strengths. What truly motivates you? What activities bring you joy and fulfillment? What unique talents do you possess? Answering these questions will provide you with a deeper understanding of who you are at your core, paving the way for a more purposeful and fulfilling career path.

As you delve into your inner landscape, you might encounter limiting beliefs that have held you back in the past. These beliefs, often stemming from societal expectations or past experiences, can act as barriers to unleashing your full potential. It is crucial to challenge these beliefs and replace them with empowering affirmations that reinforce your capabilities and worthiness.

One of the most powerful tools for unlocking your inner potential is cultivating self-belief. This involves recognizing and appreciating your unique strengths and talents, and trusting in your ability to achieve your goals. Embrace your individuality and celebrate your differences, for it is these qualities that set you apart and make you invaluable.

Another key aspect of unleashing your inner potential is continuous learning and growth. The world is constantly evolving, and so too should your skills and knowledge. Embrace a growth mindset that welcomes challenges as opportunities for learning and development. Seek out new experiences, pursue further education, and expand your skillset to remain adaptable and competitive in the ever-changing professional landscape.

In addition to personal growth, it is essential to create a supportive environment that fosters your development. Surround yourself with positive and encouraging individuals who believe in your potential and uplift you. Seek out mentors who can provide guidance and share their wisdom, as well as peers who can offer support and inspiration.

Remember, unleashing your inner potential is not a one-time event, but an ongoing process. It requires consistent effort, self-reflection, and a willingness to step outside of your comfort zone. Embrace the journey with curiosity and enthusiasm, and trust that the path you create will lead you to a career filled with meaning, purpose, and success.

As you embark on this transformative journey, it is important to celebrate your progress and acknowledge your achievements. Every step you take toward unleashing your inner potential is a victory worth recognizing. By honoring your growth and celebrating your successes, you will reinforce your self-belief and fuel your motivation to continue reaching new heights.

The journey of unleashing your inner potential is not always easy. You may encounter setbacks, obstacles, and moments of self-doubt. However, it is during these challenges that your resilience and determination will be tested and strengthened. Remember that failure is not the opposite of success, but rather a stepping stone on the path towards it. Embrace these experiences as opportunities for learning and growth, and allow them to propel you forward with even greater determination.

In conclusion, unleashing your inner potential is a transformative process that requires self-discovery, self-belief, continuous learning, and a supportive environment. It is a journey that is unique to each individual, and the rewards are immeasurable. By embracing your authentic self, cultivating your strengths, and pursuing your passions, you will unlock a world of possibilities and create a career that is both fulfilling and impactful. Remember, your potential is limitless, and it is within your power to unleash it and create the life you desire.

ppp

Your career is a canvas, and you are the artist. Unleash your inner potential, paint with bold strokes of ambition, and create a masterpiece that reflects your unique brilliance.

TWO

BUILDING CONFIDENCE FROM WITHIN

Confidence isn't a switch to be flipped on and off at will. It's a muscle that grows stronger with consistent exercise and care. Building confidence from within is a journey, not a destination, and it's essential for women who seek to master their careers.

Authentic confidence starts with self-awareness. Understanding your strengths, weaknesses, values, and passions is the foundation upon which genuine confidence is built. Take the time to reflect on your accomplishments, both big and small. Celebrate your wins and acknowledge the skills and qualities that led to your successes. Recognize the unique value you bring to the table and the contributions you make to your workplace and community.

Self-compassion is a crucial component of building confidence from within. We all make mistakes, face setbacks, and experience moments of self-doubt. It's essential to treat yourself with kindness and understanding during these times. Remember that everyone struggles, and it's okay to not be perfect. Learn from your mistakes and use them as opportunities for growth, rather than dwelling on them and allowing them to erode your confidence.

Positive self-talk is another powerful tool for cultivating confidence. The way you talk to yourself has a significant impact on your self-esteem and beliefs. Challenge negative thoughts and replace them with affirmations that reinforce your strengths and abilities. Practice speaking to yourself with kindness and encouragement, just as you would to a friend or loved one. Over time, positive self-talk can rewire your brain and foster a more optimistic and confident outlook.

Setting and achieving goals is a fundamental aspect of building confidence. Start with small, achievable goals that align with your values and aspirations. As you accomplish these goals, your confidence will naturally grow, and you'll feel empowered to tackle bigger challenges. Celebrate your successes along the way, and use them as stepping stones towards larger ambitions.

Stepping outside of your comfort zone is essential for personal and professional growth. Embracing new challenges and experiences can help you develop new skills, expand your knowledge, and build resilience. Don't be afraid to try new things, even if they seem daunting at first. The more you push yourself beyond your limits, the more confident you'll become in your abilities.

Surrounding yourself with positive and supportive people is crucial for building confidence. Seek out individuals who uplift and encourage you, and distance yourself from those who bring you down. Build a network of mentors, peers, and friends who believe in you and your potential. Their support and encouragement can provide a valuable boost to your confidence during challenging times.

Remember, building confidence is an ongoing process. It requires patience, perseverance, and a commitment to self-improvement. Don't get discouraged by setbacks or moments of self-doubt. Instead, use them as opportunities to learn, grow, and strengthen your resolve. Focus on your progress, celebrate your successes, and trust in your ability to achieve your goals.

Embrace your imperfections and vulnerabilities. They are what make you human and relatable. Don't strive for perfection; instead, strive for authenticity and continuous growth. Remember, confidence is not about being flawless; it's about embracing your whole self, with all of your strengths and weaknesses.

By cultivating self-awareness, practicing self-compassion, engaging in positive self-talk, setting and achieving goals, stepping outside of your comfort zone, and surrounding yourself with supportive people, you can build unshakeable confidence from within. This inner confidence will empower you to pursue your dreams, overcome challenges, and achieve your full potential in both your personal and professional life. It will radiate outwards, inspiring others and opening doors to new opportunities. Remember, the journey of building confidence is a lifelong adventure, and the rewards are immeasurable.

ppp

Confidence is not about being flawless; it's about embracing your whole self, with all your strengths and imperfections. Cultivate self-belief from within, and watch your career soar to new heights.

THREE

SETTING POWERFUL CAREER GOALS

In the intricate tapestry of career development, setting powerful goals emerges as a cornerstone, a guiding star that illuminates the path towards mastery. It's more than simply wishing or dreaming; it's a deliberate act of envisioning your desired future and charting a course to reach it. For women navigating the complexities of the professional world, establishing clear, meaningful, and achievable career goals is a critical step towards fulfilling their potential and creating a legacy of success.

The first step in setting powerful career goals is introspection. Take the time to delve deep into your aspirations and desires. What truly motivates you? What kind of impact do you want to make in your field? What skills do you wish to acquire, and what challenges do you aspire to conquer? By understanding your passions and values, you can align your goals with your authentic self, creating a sense of purpose that fuels your journey.

Once you've clarified your inner compass, it's time to translate your aspirations into concrete, actionable goals. These goals should be specific, measurable, achievable, relevant, and time-bound – the SMART framework. For example, instead of a vague goal like "advance in my career," a SMART goal might be "get promoted to senior manager within two years by developing leadership skills and exceeding performance targets." This specificity provides a clear roadmap and enables you to track your progress, making adjustments as needed.

While long-term goals paint a picture of your ultimate destination, short-term goals serve as stepping stones along the way. These smaller milestones create a sense of accomplishment and build momentum, keeping you motivated and engaged. Think of short-term goals as mini-experiments that allow you to test different paths and refine your direction. They also provide opportunities to learn and grow, equipping you with the skills and knowledge necessary to achieve your larger aspirations.

Flexibility is key in the realm of goal-setting. The professional landscape is constantly evolving, and unexpected opportunities or challenges may arise. Be willing to adapt your goals as circumstances change, without losing sight of your overall vision. Remember, the journey to career mastery is not always a straight line; it's often a winding path with unexpected turns and detours. Embrace the uncertainty and remain open to new possibilities.

The power of visualization cannot be underestimated in the pursuit of your goals. Take time each day to vividly imagine yourself achieving your desired outcomes. Feel the emotions associated with success, visualize the steps you need to take, and internalize the belief that your goals are attainable. This mental rehearsal can strengthen your resolve, boost your confidence, and program your subconscious mind for success.

Accountability is another crucial ingredient in the recipe for goal achievement. Share your goals with trusted mentors, colleagues, or friends who can offer support and encouragement. Consider joining a professional development group or finding an accountability partner who shares similar aspirations. By creating a network of support, you'll be more likely to stay on track and overcome obstacles that may arise along the way.

Regularly reviewing and adjusting your goals is essential for maintaining momentum and ensuring alignment with your evolving aspirations. Set aside time each month or quarter to reflect on your progress, celebrate your achievements, and identify areas where you may need to modify your approach. This process of self-assessment allows you to stay focused, motivated, and adaptable in the face of change.

Don't be afraid to dream big and set ambitious goals. While it's important to be realistic, don't let fear or self-doubt limit your potential. Push your boundaries, challenge yourself, and embrace the unknown. Remember, your goals are not just about achieving external success; they're about personal growth, fulfillment, and making a meaningful contribution to the world.

In the grand symphony of your career, setting powerful goals is the conductor's baton, orchestrating a harmonious blend of passion, purpose, and perseverance. By clarifying your aspirations, translating them into SMART goals, embracing flexibility, utilizing visualization, cultivating accountability, and regularly reviewing your progress, you can create a roadmap for success that will guide you towards career mastery and a life filled with meaning and purpose.

ppp

Don't just dream about your career; design it. Set powerful goals, create a roadmap for success, and embrace the journey with unwavering determination.

FOUR

Navigating Workplace Dynamics

The modern workplace is a dynamic, complex ecosystem. It's a place where diverse personalities, ambitions, and communication styles converge, creating a tapestry of interactions that can either propel you forward or hold you back. For women aspiring to career mastery, navigating these workplace dynamics is an essential skill. It requires emotional intelligence, astute observation, and a nuanced understanding of the unwritten rules that govern professional relationships.

At its core, navigating workplace dynamics involves building strong relationships with colleagues, supervisors, and stakeholders. This doesn't mean being everyone's best friend, but rather cultivating a network of allies who respect your work, value your contributions, and support your career aspirations. These relationships can provide invaluable insights, mentorship opportunities, and a sense of belonging within the organization.

One of the most critical aspects of navigating workplace dynamics is effective communication. This involves not only expressing your ideas clearly and persuasively but also listening actively to others. Understand that communication is a two-way street, and strive to create a dialogue where everyone feels heard and valued. Be mindful of your nonverbal cues, such as body language and tone of voice, as they can convey as much meaning as your words.

In any workplace, conflicts are inevitable. However, how you approach and resolve these conflicts can significantly impact your career trajectory. Instead of viewing conflicts as obstacles, see them as opportunities for growth and understanding. Seek to understand the underlying issues, listen to different perspectives, and work collaboratively to find solutions that benefit all parties involved. Remember, a win-win outcome is often more sustainable and fosters a positive work environment.

Navigating workplace politics is a delicate dance that requires tact, diplomacy, and a keen understanding of power dynamics. It's essential to be aware of the unspoken rules and alliances that exist within your organization, without compromising your integrity or values. By building relationships with key stakeholders and understanding their motivations, you can influence decisions, advocate for your ideas, and navigate potential obstacles.

Mentorship can be a powerful tool for navigating workplace dynamics. Seek out seasoned professionals who can offer guidance, share their experiences, and provide valuable insights into the unwritten rules of your industry or organization. A mentor can help you navigate challenges, identify opportunities, and accelerate your career growth. Conversely, consider becoming a mentor yourself. Sharing your knowledge and experience can not only benefit others but also strengthen your leadership skills and professional network.

In the digital age, navigating virtual workplace dynamics is becoming increasingly important. With remote work and virtual teams becoming the norm, building rapport and trust through online communication requires additional effort. Be proactive in reaching out to colleagues, schedule virtual coffee chats, and participate in online social events. Use video conferencing whenever possible to foster a sense of connection and build relationships.

Understanding and adapting to different communication styles is crucial in the workplace. Some individuals are direct and assertive, while others are more reserved and indirect. By recognizing these differences and adjusting your communication approach accordingly, you can avoid misunderstandings, build stronger relationships, and foster a more inclusive work environment.

Managing up is a crucial skill for navigating workplace dynamics. This involves understanding your supervisor's communication style, priorities, and expectations, and tailoring your approach accordingly. Keep your supervisor informed about your progress, seek their feedback, and proactively offer solutions to challenges. By building a strong relationship with your supervisor, you can gain their trust, support, and advocacy.

Self-advocacy is another key aspect of navigating workplace dynamics. Don't be afraid to speak up for yourself, share your ideas, and negotiate for what you deserve. Be confident in your abilities, articulate your accomplishments, and advocate for your professional development. By actively managing your career and advocating for your needs, you can create opportunities for growth and advancement.

Navigating workplace dynamics is an ongoing process that requires continuous learning, adaptation, and self-awareness. By building strong relationships, communicating effectively, resolving conflicts constructively, understanding office politics, seeking mentorship, and embracing diversity, you can create a positive and productive work environment that supports your career aspirations. Remember, the workplace is a dynamic ecosystem, and your ability to navigate its complexities is a testament to your resilience, adaptability, and leadership potential.

ᐅᐅᐅ

The workplace is a dynamic ecosystem, filled with diverse personalities and hidden agendas. Master the art of navigation, build strong relationships, and communicate with impact and influence.

FIVE

MASTERING THE ART OF NETWORKING

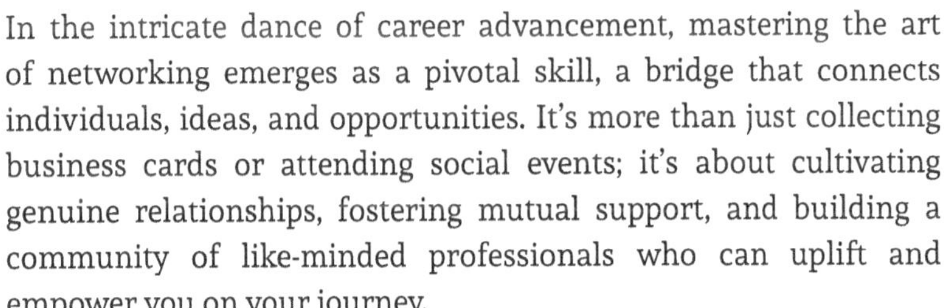

In the intricate dance of career advancement, mastering the art of networking emerges as a pivotal skill, a bridge that connects individuals, ideas, and opportunities. It's more than just collecting business cards or attending social events; it's about cultivating genuine relationships, fostering mutual support, and building a community of like-minded professionals who can uplift and empower you on your journey.

At its core, networking is about creating authentic connections. It's about seeing the people behind the titles, understanding their aspirations, and finding common ground. Approach networking with a genuine interest in others, and be willing to share your own story, experiences, and expertise. Remember, networking is a two-way street, and the most valuable connections are built on mutual respect, trust, and reciprocity.

Building a strong network takes time and effort. It's not about attending a single event or adding a few names to your contact list. It's about nurturing relationships over time, staying in touch, and offering support and encouragement. Make a conscious effort to connect with people regularly, whether through coffee chats, informational interviews, or virtual gatherings. Be proactive in sharing relevant articles, job postings, or industry insights, and celebrate the successes of others in your network.

One of the most powerful aspects of networking is its ability to open doors to new opportunities. A well-cultivated network can provide access to information, resources, and introductions that might otherwise be difficult to obtain. It can lead to job offers, mentorship opportunities, collaborations, and even lifelong friendships. However, it's important to remember that networking is not just about what others can do for you; it's also about what you can offer them. Be generous with your time, expertise, and connections, and be willing to pay it forward.

In the digital age, online networking has become increasingly important. Platforms like LinkedIn, Twitter, and professional forums offer a vast array of opportunities to connect with people from all over the world. Utilize these platforms to expand your reach, join relevant groups, participate in discussions, and share your insights. However, don't neglect the power of in-person networking. Attending industry events, conferences, and workshops can provide valuable face-to-face interactions and build deeper connections.

When networking, it's essential to be mindful of your personal brand. This includes your online presence, your appearance, your communication style, and the overall impression you leave on others. Be intentional about how you present yourself, and strive to be authentic, professional, and memorable. A strong personal brand can enhance your credibility, attract opportunities, and open doors to new connections.

Networking is not just about quantity; it's about quality. It's better to have a few deep, meaningful connections than a large network of superficial acquaintances. Focus on building relationships with people who share your values, interests, and career aspirations. These connections will be more likely to offer support, guidance, and opportunities that align with your goals.

Don't be afraid to step outside of your comfort zone and connect with people who are different from you. Diversity is a strength, and building a diverse network can expose you to new perspectives, ideas, and opportunities. Seek out individuals from different backgrounds, industries, and experience levels. You might be surprised by the connections you make and the insights you gain.

Remember, networking is a lifelong journey. It's about building a community of support, fostering mutual growth, and creating a legacy of impact. By approaching networking with authenticity, generosity, and a willingness to learn and grow, you can unlock a world of possibilities and achieve career mastery on your own terms.

Networking is not a one-size-fits-all endeavor. It's important to find strategies that work for you and align with your personality and preferences. Some people thrive in large social gatherings, while others prefer one-on-one interactions. Experiment with different approaches and find what feels most natural and authentic for you.

Finally, don't forget to follow up and nurture your connections. A simple thank-you note, a follow-up email, or a LinkedIn message can go a long way in building rapport and strengthening relationships. Stay in touch with your network regularly, offer support when needed, and celebrate their successes. By investing in your relationships, you're investing in your future.

Mastering the art of networking is a journey, not a destination.

It requires patience, persistence, and a genuine desire to connect with others. By embracing networking as a tool for personal and professional growth, you can open doors to new opportunities, build a supportive community, and create a legacy of impact that will last a lifetime.

Your network is your net worth. Cultivate authentic connections, nurture relationships, and build a community of support that will uplift and empower you on your career journey.

SIX

COMMUNICATING WITH IMPACT AND INFLUENCE

Communicating with impact and influence is a skill that transcends industries, roles, and hierarchies. It's a skill that empowers individuals to not just convey information but to inspire action, shape opinions, and drive meaningful change. For women in the workplace, mastering this skill is essential for career advancement, leadership, and making a lasting impact on their organizations and communities.

At its core, impactful communication begins with clarity. Before crafting a message, it's crucial to define your purpose and understand your audience. What do you want to achieve with your communication? What information does your audience need, and what are their interests and concerns? By tailoring your message to resonate with your listeners, you'll increase the likelihood of capturing their attention and inspiring them to take action.

Crafting a compelling narrative is a powerful way to communicate with impact. Stories engage our emotions, tap into our values, and make information more relatable and memorable. Whether you're pitching an idea, giving a presentation, or simply conversing with a colleague, incorporating storytelling elements can enhance your message and leave a lasting impression.

Effective communication involves not only what you say but also how you say it. Your tone of voice, body language, and facial expressions all contribute to the overall impact of your message. Be mindful of your nonverbal cues and ensure they align with your words. A confident posture, direct eye contact, and a genuine smile can convey authority, trustworthiness, and enthusiasm.

Active listening is a critical component of impactful communication. It involves not just hearing the words spoken but also understanding the underlying message and emotions. When you actively listen, you demonstrate respect, build rapport, and gather valuable insights that can inform your response. Ask clarifying questions, summarize what you've heard, and validate the speaker's feelings. By truly listening, you create a space for open dialogue and collaboration.

In a world inundated with information, cutting through the noise requires concise and focused communication. Avoid jargon, clichés, and unnecessary details. Instead, distill your message to its essence and deliver it with precision and impact. Use strong verbs, vivid imagery, and impactful language to capture your audience's attention and leave a lasting impression.

Persuasion is an art that involves understanding your audience's motivations, values, and concerns. Tailor your message to appeal to their interests and address their needs. Use evidence, data, and examples to support your arguments and demonstrate the value of your ideas. Be confident, enthusiastic, and passionate about your message. Your conviction will be contagious and inspire others to rally behind your cause.

Adaptability is key in communication. Be willing to adjust your style and approach based on your audience and the situation. For example, a formal presentation might require a different tone and level of detail than a casual conversation with a colleague. By being flexible and adaptable, you can effectively communicate with diverse audiences and navigate various communication channels.

Effective communication is not just about transmitting information; it's about building relationships and fostering trust. Be authentic, transparent, and approachable. Show genuine interest in others, ask thoughtful questions, and actively listen to their responses. By cultivating strong relationships, you'll create a network of allies who trust and respect you, making it easier to influence and inspire them.

Continuous learning and improvement are essential for mastering the art of communication. Seek out feedback from trusted colleagues, mentors, or coaches. Observe effective communicators in your field and learn from their techniques. Attend workshops, seminars, or online courses to enhance your communication skills. By investing in your development, you'll become a more impactful and influential communicator.

Remember, communication is a journey, not a destination. It takes time, practice, and a willingness to learn and grow. Embrace challenges, experiment with different approaches, and learn from your mistakes. By honing your communication skills, you'll empower yourself to lead, inspire, and make a meaningful difference in your personal and professional life.

In conclusion, communicating with impact and influence is a multifaceted skill that involves clarity, storytelling, nonverbal communication, active listening, conciseness, persuasion, adaptability, relationship building, and continuous learning. By mastering these elements, you can transform your communication from mere information transfer to a powerful tool for inspiring action, driving change, and achieving your goals. Remember, effective communication is not just a skill; it's a superpower that can propel you to new heights of success and fulfillment.

ϼϼϼ

Words have the power to inspire, persuade, and transform. Hone your communication skills, speak with clarity and conviction, and leave a lasting impression on the people you encounter.

SEVEN

DEVELOPING LEADERSHIP SKILLS

Leadership is not merely a position or title; it is a mindset, a set of skills, and a way of being that empowers individuals to inspire and guide others towards a common vision. For women in the workplace, developing strong leadership skills is essential for breaking barriers, shattering stereotypes, and achieving career mastery. It's about stepping up, taking charge, and creating a positive impact on your organization and community.

At the heart of leadership lies the ability to inspire and motivate others. Great leaders have a clear vision for the future, and they communicate that vision with passion and conviction. They empower their teams to reach their full potential, fostering a sense of shared purpose and ownership. They celebrate successes, learn from failures, and create a culture of continuous improvement.

Effective communication is a cornerstone of leadership. Leaders must be able to articulate their ideas clearly, listen actively to feedback, and build consensus among diverse stakeholders. They understand the power of storytelling, using narratives to connect with their audience, evoke emotions, and inspire action. They also know how to adapt their communication style to different situations and audiences, ensuring that their message resonates with everyone.

Building strong relationships is another critical aspect of leadership. Leaders invest time and energy in getting to know their team members, understanding their strengths and weaknesses, and fostering a sense of trust and respect. They create a supportive and inclusive environment where everyone feels valued and empowered to contribute their best work. They also build relationships with external stakeholders, such as customers, partners, and community leaders, to create a network of support and collaboration.

Decision-making is a fundamental part of leadership. Leaders must be able to gather information, analyze options, and make sound decisions that align with their values and goals. They understand that not all decisions will be popular, but they have the courage to stand by their convictions and take responsibility for the outcomes. They also empower their teams to make decisions, fostering a culture of autonomy and accountability.

Problem-solving is a critical skill for leaders. They approach challenges with a growth mindset, viewing them as opportunities for learning and improvement. They break down complex problems into manageable steps, gather relevant information, and explore creative solutions. They involve their team in the problem-solving process, tapping into their collective knowledge and expertise.

Adaptability is essential in today's rapidly changing world. Leaders must be able to pivot quickly, embrace new technologies, and adapt to evolving market conditions. They encourage their teams to be flexible and open to change, fostering a culture of innovation and experimentation. They also model adaptability by embracing lifelong learning and staying abreast of the latest trends and developments in their field.

Resilience is the ability to bounce back from setbacks and challenges. Leaders understand that failure is a natural part of the learning process, and they use it as a stepping stone to success. They maintain a positive attitude, persevere in the face of adversity, and inspire their teams to do the same. They also create a culture of psychological safety where team members feel comfortable taking risks and learning from their mistakes.

Ethical leadership is about making decisions that are not only legally sound but also morally right. Leaders act with integrity, honesty, and transparency. They treat their employees, customers, and partners with respect and fairness. They also hold themselves accountable for their actions and strive to create a positive impact on society.

Developing leadership skills is an ongoing journey. It requires self-awareness, a willingness to learn, and a commitment to personal and professional growth. Seek out opportunities to lead, whether it's heading a project at work, volunteering in your community, or mentoring a younger colleague. Embrace challenges, learn from your mistakes, and celebrate your successes. By continuously developing your leadership skills, you'll empower yourself to create a lasting impact and achieve your full potential.

Remember, leadership is not about being perfect; it's about being human. It's about recognizing your strengths and weaknesses, learning from others, and inspiring those around you to reach their full potential. By embracing the journey of leadership, you'll not only transform your own life but also make a positive impact on the world.

ᗐᗐᗐ

Leadership is not about titles or positions; it's about inspiring and empowering others to reach their full potential. Embrace your leadership potential, foster a culture of collaboration, and leave a lasting legacy of impact.

EIGHT

NEGOTIATING FOR YOUR WORTH

Negotiating for your worth is a critical skill that can significantly impact your career trajectory and financial well-being. It's about advocating for yourself, recognizing your value, and ensuring that you are fairly compensated for your contributions. For women, who often face systemic barriers and biases in the workplace, mastering the art of negotiation is especially crucial. It's a way to bridge the gender pay gap, achieve equal pay for equal work, and create a more equitable professional landscape.

The first step in negotiating for your worth is to know your value. This involves researching industry standards, salary surveys, and comparable positions to determine a fair market value for your skills and experience. Consider your unique qualifications, accomplishments, and the value you bring to your organization. Don't underestimate your worth or sell yourself short. Remember, you have valuable skills and experience that deserve to be recognized and rewarded.

Preparation is key to successful negotiation. Before entering any negotiation, thoroughly research the company, the position, and the industry. Understand the company's culture, values, and compensation philosophy. Identify your key selling points and be prepared to articulate them clearly and confidently. Practice your negotiation script, anticipating potential questions and objections. The more prepared you are, the more confident you'll feel during the negotiation process.

Confidence is crucial in negotiation. Believe in your worth and your ability to negotiate a fair outcome. Project confidence through your body language, tone of voice, and overall demeanor. Remember, you're not asking for a favor; you're advocating for fair compensation based on your skills and experience. Be assertive, but not aggressive. Maintain a professional and respectful tone throughout the negotiation process.

Negotiation is a dialogue, not a monologue. Be prepared to listen actively to the other party's perspective, concerns, and constraints. Seek to understand their needs and interests. Be open to compromise and creative solutions that benefit both parties. Remember, negotiation is not about winning or losing; it's about reaching a mutually agreeable outcome that satisfies everyone involved.

Don't be afraid to ask for what you want. Be clear and specific about your salary expectations, benefits, and other terms of employment. Don't settle for less than you deserve. Remember, the first offer is often just a starting point. Be prepared to counteroffer and negotiate until you reach a fair and equitable agreement.

Timing is crucial in negotiation. Choose a time when the other party is most likely to be receptive to your request. For example, after you've received a job offer or after you've demonstrated exceptional performance. Avoid negotiating when the other party is stressed, distracted, or facing a deadline.

Negotiation is not just about money. Consider the entire

compensation package, including benefits, bonuses, stock options, vacation time, and flexible work arrangements. Think about your priorities and what matters most to you. Be prepared to negotiate on multiple fronts to achieve a package that meets your needs and goals.

Negotiation is a learned skill. The more you practice, the better you'll become at it. Seek out opportunities to negotiate in various aspects of your life, such as salary, promotions, contracts, and even everyday purchases. Learn from your experiences, both successes and failures. With practice, you'll develop the confidence and skills to negotiate effectively for your worth.

Overcoming fear and self-doubt is essential for successful negotiation. Many women hesitate to negotiate because they fear being perceived as greedy or aggressive. Remember, negotiating is not a sign of greed; it's a sign of self-respect and a commitment to your professional worth. Don't let fear hold you back. Embrace negotiation as an opportunity to advocate for yourself and achieve your full potential.

Remember, negotiating for your worth is an ongoing process. It's not a one-time event, but a continuous effort to ensure that you are fairly compensated for your contributions. Don't be afraid to renegotiate your salary or benefits as your skills, experience, and responsibilities grow. By consistently advocating for yourself, you'll not only achieve greater financial success but also empower yourself and other women in the workplace.

▷▷▷

Your worth is not determined by others; it's a reflection of your unique skills, experience, and value you bring to the table. Negotiate with confidence, advocate for your worth, and never settle for less than you deserve.

NINE

FINDING MENTORSHIP AND SPONSORSHIP

In the intricate landscape of career advancement, mentorship and sponsorship emerge as guiding lights, illuminating the path towards mastery and fulfillment. They are the compass that helps women navigate the often-uncharted territories of professional growth, providing invaluable support, guidance, and advocacy. In this exploration, we delve into the transformative power of mentorship and sponsorship, uncovering their distinct roles, the profound impact they can have on a woman's career, and the strategies for cultivating these invaluable relationships.

Mentorship, at its core, is a relationship built on trust, mutual respect, and a shared desire for growth. A mentor is a seasoned professional who offers guidance, advice, and support to a less experienced individual, known as a mentee. This relationship can be formal or informal, structured or organic, but its essence lies in the exchange of knowledge, insights, and perspectives.

A mentor serves as a sounding board, offering a safe space for the mentee to explore ideas, challenges, and aspirations. They share their experiences, wisdom, and lessons learned, helping the mentee navigate the complexities of the professional world. They provide feedback, offer encouragement, and challenge the mentee to step outside their comfort zone and reach their full potential.

The benefits of mentorship are manifold. Mentees gain access to a wealth of knowledge and experience, accelerating their learning and development. They receive guidance on navigating workplace dynamics, building relationships, and making strategic career decisions. They also benefit from the mentor's network and connections, opening doors to new opportunities and collaborations.

Sponsorship, on the other hand, takes mentorship a step further. A sponsor is a senior-level executive who not only provides guidance and support but also actively advocates for the career advancement of their protégé. They leverage their influence and network to create opportunities, champion their protégé's accomplishments, and open doors that might otherwise remain closed.

Sponsorship is a powerful tool for women, who often face systemic barriers and biases in the workplace. A sponsor can help level the playing field by providing access to key decision-makers, advocating for promotions and raises, and ensuring that their protégé's contributions are recognized and rewarded. They also serve as role models, demonstrating what is possible and inspiring their protégé to reach new heights.

Cultivating mentorship and sponsorship relationships requires intentionality and effort. Start by identifying potential mentors and sponsors within your organization or industry. Look for individuals who have achieved success in areas that align with your career aspirations. Attend industry events, conferences, and workshops to expand your network and connect with potential mentors and sponsors.

When approaching potential mentors or sponsors, be clear about your goals and what you hope to gain from the relationship. Express your admiration for their work and explain why you believe they would be a valuable mentor or sponsor. Be prepared to offer something in return, such as your time, expertise, or willingness to learn.

Once you've established a mentorship or sponsorship relationship, nurture it with regular communication, gratitude, and reciprocity. Keep your mentor or sponsor updated on your progress, seek their feedback, and express your appreciation for their support. Be willing to offer your own insights and perspectives, and don't hesitate to ask for help when needed.

Remember, mentorship and sponsorship are not one-way streets. They are partnerships built on mutual respect, trust, and a shared desire for growth. By investing in these relationships, you're investing in your own future. You're opening yourself up to new possibilities, expanding your network, and accelerating your career trajectory.

In conclusion, mentorship and sponsorship are invaluable resources for women seeking career mastery. They provide guidance, support, advocacy, and access to opportunities that can propel you towards your goals. By actively seeking out mentors and sponsors, nurturing those relationships, and paying it forward, you can create a ripple effect of empowerment and create a more equitable and inclusive workplace for all. Remember, your career journey is not a solo endeavor. With the right mentors and sponsors by your side, you can achieve your full potential and make a lasting impact on the world.

ϷϷϷ

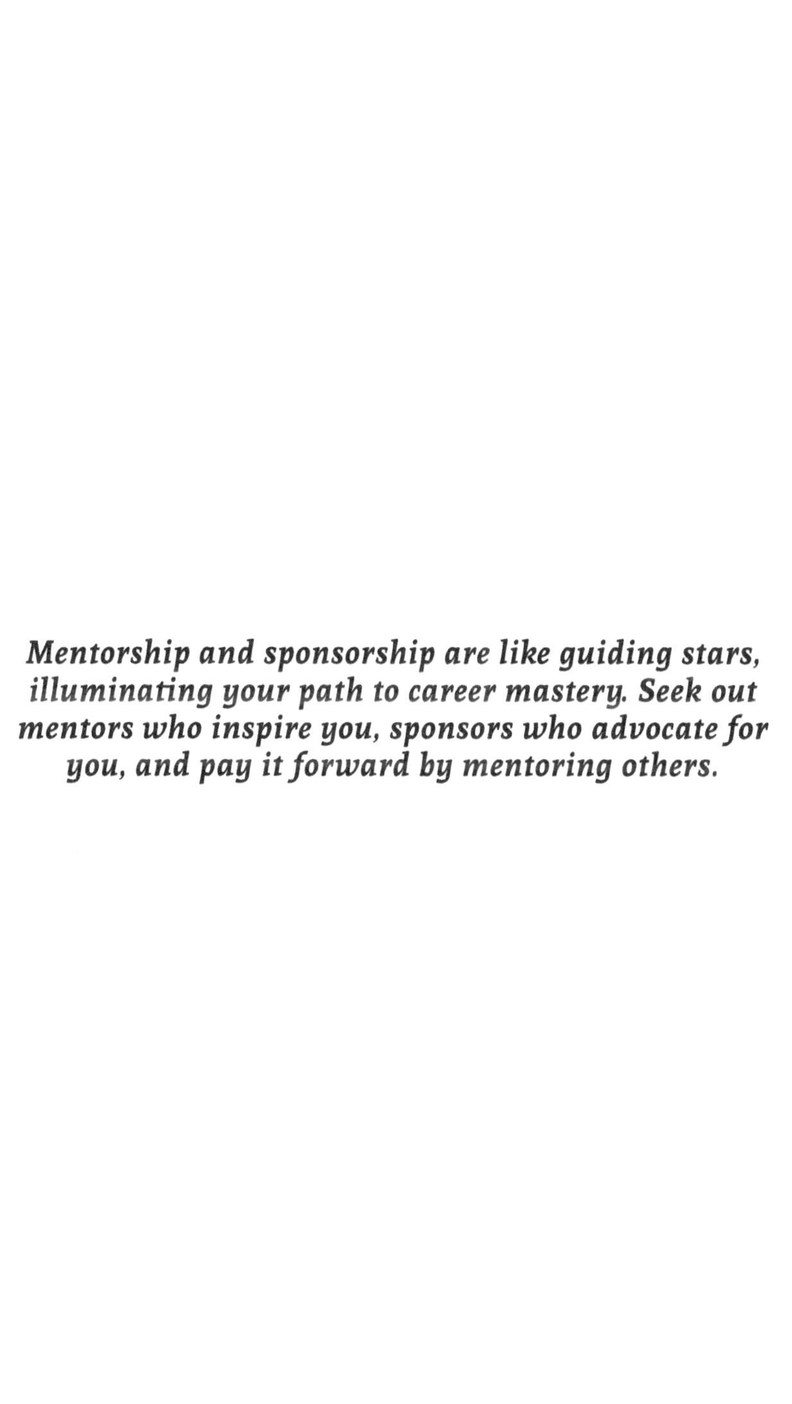

Mentorship and sponsorship are like guiding stars, illuminating your path to career mastery. Seek out mentors who inspire you, sponsors who advocate for you, and pay it forward by mentoring others.

TEN

BUILDING YOUR PERSONAL BRAND

In the vast and competitive professional landscape, building a personal brand has emerged as a powerful tool for women to distinguish themselves, amplify their impact, and achieve career mastery. It's more than just self-promotion; it's a strategic process of defining, communicating, and consistently embodying your unique value proposition. It's about crafting a narrative that resonates with your target audience, establishing your expertise, and leaving a lasting impression on the people you encounter.

At the heart of personal branding lies self-discovery. Before you can effectively communicate your brand to the world, you need to have a deep understanding of who you are, what you stand for, and what sets you apart. Take the time to reflect on your values, passions, skills, and experiences. Identify your strengths and weaknesses, your unique perspectives, and your areas of expertise. This self-awareness will serve as the foundation upon which you build your personal brand.

Once you've clarified your identity, it's time to define your brand message. What do you want to be known for? What are the key messages you want to convey about yourself and your work? Your brand message should be concise, compelling, and authentic. It should reflect your values, your expertise, and the impact you want to make in the world.

Crafting a strong online presence is essential for building your personal brand in the digital age. Your online profiles, such as LinkedIn, Twitter, and personal websites, serve as your digital storefront. Ensure that they are up-to-date, professional, and consistent with your brand message. Use high-quality headshots, write compelling bios, and showcase your accomplishments and expertise.

Creating valuable content is a powerful way to establish your expertise and build your personal brand. Share your insights, knowledge, and experiences through blog posts, articles, social media updates, or even videos. Be consistent in your messaging and strive to provide value to your audience. By sharing your expertise, you position yourself as a thought leader in your field and attract a loyal following.

Networking is a crucial component of personal branding. Actively engage with your professional network, both online and offline. Attend industry events, conferences, and workshops. Connect with colleagues, mentors, and potential clients on LinkedIn and other social media platforms. Build relationships based on mutual respect, trust, and reciprocity. By expanding your network and fostering meaningful connections, you'll increase your visibility and create opportunities for collaboration and growth.

Consistency is key in personal branding. Ensure that your brand message, online presence, and professional interactions are all aligned and consistent. This means communicating your brand message consistently across all channels, maintaining a professional demeanor, and delivering on your promises. Consistency builds trust, credibility, and recognition, which are essential for a strong personal brand.

Authenticity is the cornerstone of personal branding. Be genuine, transparent, and true to yourself. Don't try to be someone you're not. Instead, embrace your unique personality, quirks, and experiences. People are drawn to authenticity, and it's what will ultimately set you apart from the competition.

Building a personal brand takes time, effort, and dedication. It's an ongoing process of self-discovery, refinement, and evolution. Don't be afraid to experiment, try new things, and learn from your mistakes. Seek feedback from trusted colleagues, mentors, or coaches to gain valuable insights and improve your approach.

Remember, your personal brand is not just about what you say or do; it's about who you are and the impact you make on the world. By building a strong personal brand, you'll empower yourself to achieve your career goals, make a meaningful contribution to your field, and leave a lasting legacy. Embrace the journey of personal branding with passion, authenticity, and a commitment to excellence, and watch your career soar to new heights.

ϷϷϷ

Your personal brand is your unique value proposition. Craft a compelling narrative, establish your expertise, and consistently embody your brand in every interaction.

ELEVEN

BALANCING CAREER AND PERSONAL LIFE

In the modern era, the pursuit of a fulfilling career and a thriving personal life often feels like a delicate balancing act. The demands of work, family, relationships, and personal well-being can pull us in different directions, leaving us feeling overwhelmed, stressed, and disconnected. Especially for women, who often shoulder the majority of caregiving responsibilities, finding a harmonious balance between career and personal life can seem like an elusive dream. However, with intentional effort, thoughtful strategies, and a commitment to self-care, achieving a fulfilling and sustainable balance is indeed possible.

The first step in achieving work-life balance is to redefine what balance means to you. It's not about dividing your time equally between work and personal life, but rather about integrating the two in a way that feels fulfilling and sustainable. This requires understanding your priorities, values, and goals, both personally and professionally. What matters most to you? What activities bring you joy and fulfillment? What are your non-negotiables in terms of time spent with loved ones, pursuing hobbies, or simply taking time for yourself?

Once you've clarified your priorities, it's time to set boundaries. This means establishing clear boundaries between work and personal life. It might involve setting specific work hours, limiting after-hours emails and calls, and creating dedicated time for family, friends, and personal activities. It also means learning to say no to additional commitments that don't align with your priorities or values.

Time management is a crucial skill for achieving work-life balance. Learn to prioritize tasks, delegate responsibilities, and eliminate unnecessary distractions. Use tools like calendars, to-do lists, and time-tracking apps to stay organized and focused. Schedule regular breaks throughout the day to recharge and avoid burnout. By managing your time effectively, you can maximize your productivity at work and still have time and energy for your personal life.

Self-care is an essential component of work-life balance. It's about taking care of your physical, mental, and emotional well-being. This might involve regular exercise, healthy eating, getting enough sleep, practicing mindfulness, and engaging in activities that bring you joy. When you're well-rested and energized, you're better equipped to handle the demands of both work and personal life.

Flexibility is key in the pursuit of work-life balance. Embrace flexible work arrangements whenever possible, such as telecommuting, flextime, or compressed workweeks. These arrangements can provide greater control over your schedule and allow you to better integrate work and personal life. If your current job doesn't offer flexible options, consider exploring alternative career paths that offer greater flexibility.

Open communication is essential in both your personal and professional relationships. Talk to your partner, family, friends, and colleagues about your needs and expectations. Share your goals and challenges, and seek their support and understanding. By communicating openly and honestly, you can build stronger relationships and create a support system that helps you navigate the complexities of work-life balance.

Don't be afraid to ask for help when you need it. Delegate tasks at work, hire a babysitter or nanny, enlist the help of friends and family, or consider outsourcing household chores. Remember, you don't have to do it all alone. By seeking help and delegating responsibilities, you can free up time and energy for the things that matter most to you.

Setting realistic expectations is crucial for maintaining work-life balance. Accept that there will be times when work demands more of your attention and other times when personal life takes priority. Don't strive for perfection; instead, strive for progress. Celebrate your successes, learn from your challenges, and adjust your approach as needed.

Embrace technology as a tool for work-life balance. Utilize online collaboration tools, project management software, and communication platforms to streamline your work and improve efficiency. Automate repetitive tasks, delegate responsibilities, and leverage technology to create more time for your personal life.

Remember, achieving work-life balance is an ongoing journey, not a destination. It requires constant reassessment, adjustment, and a willingness to experiment with different approaches. Be kind to yourself, embrace flexibility, and prioritize self-care. By creating a harmonious integration of work and personal life, you can achieve greater fulfillment, happiness, and success in all areas of your life.

Remember, the pursuit of work-life balance is a personal one. There is no one-size-fits-all solution. What works for one person may not work for another. The key is to find what works best for you, your family, and your career aspirations. By prioritizing your well-being, setting boundaries, managing your time effectively, communicating openly, seeking support, and embracing flexibility, you can create a fulfilling and sustainable work-life balance that allows you to thrive both personally and professionally.

ᐱᐱᐱ

A fulfilling career and a thriving personal life are not mutually exclusive. Strive for integration, set boundaries, prioritize self-care, and create a harmonious balance that nourishes both your professional and personal aspirations.

TWELVE
OVERCOMING IMPOSTER SYNDROME

Imposter syndrome, the pervasive feeling of self-doubt and inadequacy despite external evidence of success, is a common experience for many women in the workplace. It's that nagging voice in your head that whispers, "You're not good enough," "You don't deserve this," or "You're going to be found out as a fraud." This internalized fear of being exposed as an imposter can be crippling, undermining confidence, hindering performance, and preventing women from reaching their full potential.

The first step in overcoming imposter syndrome is to acknowledge and validate your feelings. Recognize that these feelings are real and common, but they are not based on reality. Remind yourself that you are not alone in experiencing these doubts and that even the most successful people often struggle with imposter syndrome.

By acknowledging your feelings, you can begin to separate them from the facts and challenge the negative self-talk that fuels imposter syndrome.

Challenging negative self-talk is a crucial step in overcoming imposter syndrome. When you hear those critical voices in your head, counter them with positive affirmations that reinforce your strengths and accomplishments. Remind yourself of your past successes, the skills and knowledge you possess, and the positive feedback you've received from colleagues and mentors.

By actively challenging negative thoughts, you can reframe your mindset and build a more positive and empowering self-narrative.

Another powerful tool for overcoming imposter syndrome is focusing on your achievements and contributions. Keep a record of your accomplishments, both big and small. Celebrate your wins and acknowledge the value you bring to your team and organization. By focusing on your achievements, you can shift your attention away from self-doubt and towards self-efficacy.

Building a strong support network is crucial for overcoming imposter syndrome. Surround yourself with positive and encouraging individuals who believe in you and your abilities. Seek out mentors, coaches, or sponsors who can provide guidance, support, and encouragement.

Share your experiences with trusted colleagues or friends who may be able to offer a fresh perspective and help you reframe your thoughts.

Seeking professional help can also be beneficial in overcoming imposter syndrome. Therapists or counselors can help you identify the root causes of your self-doubt, develop coping mechanisms, and build a stronger sense of self-worth.

They can also provide a safe space for you to explore your feelings and develop strategies for overcoming imposter syndrome.

Reframing your perspective is another effective way to combat imposter syndrome. Instead of focusing on your perceived shortcomings, shift your attention to your strengths and potential. Embrace a growth mindset, viewing challenges and setbacks as opportunities for learning and development.

Remember, everyone makes mistakes, and failure is a natural part of the learning process. By reframing your perspective, you can turn imposter syndrome into a catalyst for growth and resilience.

Setting realistic expectations is also crucial for overcoming imposter syndrome. Don't strive for perfection; instead, strive for excellence. Remember, no one is perfect, and everyone has areas where they can improve.

Embrace your imperfections as part of what makes you unique and valuable. By setting realistic expectations, you can reduce the pressure you put on yourself and alleviate the fear of not being good enough.

Celebrate your successes and acknowledge your accomplishments. Take the time to recognize your achievements and celebrate your milestones. Reward yourself for your hard work and dedication. By celebrating your successes, you'll reinforce your self-worth and build a stronger sense of confidence in your abilities.

Remember, overcoming imposter syndrome is a journey, not a destination. It takes time, effort, and a commitment to self-improvement. Be patient with yourself, embrace self-compassion, and celebrate your progress.

By implementing these strategies and seeking support when needed, you can overcome imposter syndrome and unleash your full potential.

In conclusion, imposter syndrome is a common experience for many women in the workplace, but it doesn't have to hold you back.

By acknowledging your feelings, challenging negative self-talk, focusing on your achievements, building a strong support network, seeking professional help, reframing your perspective, setting realistic expectations, and celebrating your successes, you can overcome imposter syndrome and achieve your career goals. Remember, you are capable, you are worthy, and you deserve to succeed.

ᐁᐁᐁ

Imposter syndrome is a common but conquerable foe. Acknowledge your doubts, challenge negative self-talk, focus on your achievements, and celebrate your successes.

THIRTEEN

EMBRACING FAILURE AS A STEPPING STONE

The path to career mastery is not a smooth, linear ascent. It is often paved with setbacks, detours, and unexpected challenges. Failure is an inevitable part of the journey, an experience that can leave us feeling discouraged, demoralized, and doubting our abilities. However, reframing failure as a stepping stone rather than a stumbling block can be transformative. It can unlock new possibilities, foster resilience, and propel us towards even greater heights of success.

Embracing failure starts with a shift in perspective. Instead of viewing failure as a sign of inadequacy or incompetence, see it as an opportunity for growth and learning. Every setback, every mistake, every rejection holds valuable lessons that can inform our future decisions and actions. By analyzing our failures, identifying the root causes, and adjusting our approach, we can emerge stronger, wiser, and more resilient.

Failure can be a powerful catalyst for innovation and creativity.

When our initial attempts fall short, we are forced to think outside the box, explore new possibilities, and challenge our assumptions. This process of experimentation and exploration can lead to breakthrough ideas, novel solutions, and ultimately, greater success. Embracing failure as a stepping stone means recognizing that setbacks are not the end of the road but rather detours on the path to innovation.

Resilience, the ability to bounce back from adversity, is a key attribute of successful individuals. Failure can test our resilience, pushing us to our limits and forcing us to confront our fears and doubts. However, it is through these challenges that we develop the mental and emotional fortitude to overcome obstacles, persevere through setbacks, and ultimately achieve our goals. Embracing failure as a stepping stone means recognizing that setbacks are not permanent, and that we have the power to learn, grow, and emerge stronger from them.

Failure can also be a humbling experience, reminding us of our humanity and the importance of collaboration and support. When we fall short, we often turn to others for guidance, encouragement, and assistance. This process of seeking help and support can not only provide us with valuable insights and resources but also strengthen our relationships and build a sense of community. Embracing failure as a stepping stone means recognizing that we are not alone in our struggles and that seeking help is a sign of strength, not weakness.

Learning from failure is a critical skill for personal and professional growth. Take the time to reflect on your experiences, analyze what went wrong, and identify areas for improvement. Ask yourself: What can I learn from this? How can I do better next time? What resources or support do I need to succeed? By turning failure into a learning opportunity, you can extract valuable lessons that will inform your future decisions and actions.

Embracing failure as a stepping stone requires a growth mindset, a belief that our abilities and intelligence can be developed through dedication and hard work. It means viewing challenges as opportunities for growth, embracing feedback, and persisting in the face of setbacks. With a growth mindset, we can transform failure from a source of shame and discouragement into a catalyst for learning, innovation, and ultimately, success.

In conclusion, embracing failure as a stepping stone is a transformative mindset that can unlock new possibilities, foster resilience, and propel us towards greater heights of success. By reframing failure as an opportunity for growth, learning, innovation, and collaboration, we can harness its power to achieve our goals, overcome challenges, and create a more fulfilling and impactful career. Remember, failure is not the opposite of success; it's a stepping stone on the path towards it.

Failure is not the end of the road; it's a detour on the path to success. Embrace setbacks as learning opportunities, extract valuable lessons, and use them as stepping stones towards your goals.

FOURTEEN

CULTIVATING RESILIENCE AND ADAPTABILITY

In the ever-evolving landscape of the professional world, resilience and adaptability emerge as indispensable qualities for women who aspire to not just survive, but thrive. These twin pillars of strength enable us to navigate challenges, embrace change, and emerge from setbacks stronger and more resourceful. Cultivating resilience and adaptability is a journey of self-discovery, continuous learning, and embracing the ebb and flow of life's uncertainties.

Resilience is the capacity to withstand and recover from adversity. It's the inner strength that allows us to bounce back from setbacks, disappointments, and failures. Resilient individuals possess a strong sense of self-belief, a positive outlook, and the ability to maintain composure in the face of stress. They view challenges as opportunities for growth, embrace change as a catalyst for innovation, and persevere through adversity with unwavering determination.

Building resilience starts with self-awareness. Understanding our strengths, weaknesses, values, and triggers is crucial for developing coping mechanisms and navigating difficult situations. It also involves recognizing and managing our emotions, cultivating a positive mindset, and developing healthy habits that promote physical and mental well-being.

Adaptability, on the other hand, is the ability to adjust to new or changing circumstances. It's the capacity to embrace the unknown, pivot when necessary, and thrive in unfamiliar environments. Adaptable individuals are open to new ideas, willing to experiment, and comfortable with ambiguity. They view change as an opportunity for growth and innovation, rather than a threat to their security or status quo.

Cultivating adaptability requires a willingness to learn and evolve. It means stepping outside of our comfort zones, embracing new experiences, and seeking out opportunities to expand our skillset. It also involves developing a growth mindset, a belief that our abilities and intelligence can be developed through dedication and hard work.

Resilience and adaptability are interconnected and mutually reinforcing. When we encounter setbacks or challenges, our resilience enables us to cope with the emotional impact and bounce back stronger. Our adaptability allows us to adjust our approach, learn from our experiences, and find new ways to succeed. Together, resilience and adaptability create a powerful combination that enables us to navigate the complexities of life and achieve our goals.

In the workplace, resilience and adaptability are essential for career success. They enable us to overcome obstacles, manage stress, adapt to change, and thrive in a competitive environment. Resilient and adaptable individuals are more likely to be seen as valuable assets to their organizations, as they possess the ability to navigate challenges, embrace change, and contribute to a positive and productive work environment.

Cultivating resilience and adaptability is an ongoing process that requires continuous learning, self-reflection, and a willingness to embrace discomfort. It's about developing a toolkit of coping mechanisms, building a supportive network, and fostering a positive mindset. It's also about recognizing that setbacks and failures are not the end of the road, but rather opportunities for growth and transformation.

In conclusion, cultivating resilience and adaptability is a journey of self-discovery, continuous learning, and embracing the ebb and flow of life's uncertainties. By developing these essential qualities, we can navigate challenges, embrace change, and emerge from setbacks stronger and more resourceful. Resilience and adaptability are not just skills; they are mindsets that empower us to thrive in the face of adversity, achieve our goals, and create a fulfilling and impactful life.

ϷϷϷ

The only constant in life is change. Cultivate resilience and adaptability, embrace new challenges, and continuously learn and grow to thrive in an ever-evolving work landscape.

FIFTEEN

PROMOTING DIVERSITY AND INCLUSION

Promoting diversity and inclusion is a fundamental pillar in the pursuit of a thriving and equitable workplace. It goes beyond mere compliance with regulations; it's a conscious effort to create aculture where everyone feels valued, respected, and empowered to contribute their unique perspectives and talents. This commitment to diversity and inclusion not only enriches the workplace but also fuels innovation, enhances problem-solving capabilities, and ultimately drives organizational success.

Diversity encompasses a wide range of human experiences, including race, ethnicity, gender, sexual orientation, age, disability, religion, socioeconomic status, and more. It's about recognizing and appreciating the richness of human differences and leveraging them to create a more vibrant and dynamic workplace. Inclusion, on the other hand, is about creating an environment where everyone feels welcome, respected, and empowered to participate fully. It's about ensuring that all voices are heard, all perspectives are valued, and everyone has the opportunity to contribute their unique talents and skills.

Promoting diversity and inclusion is not just a moral imperative; it's a business imperative. Research has consistently shown that diverse teams are more innovative, creative, and better at problem-solving than homogeneous teams. They are also more likely to understand and connect with diverse customer bases, leading to increased market share and profitability. Moreover, a diverse and inclusive workplace fosters employee engagement, satisfaction, and retention, reducing turnover costs and enhancing overall productivity.

Creating a diverse and inclusive workplace starts with leadership commitment. Leaders must set the tone from the top, clearly articulating the importance of diversity and inclusion and demonstrating their commitment through their actions. This includes establishing clear goals and metrics, holding themselves and others accountable, and embedding diversity and inclusion into the organization's values, policies, and practices.

Recruitment and hiring practices play a critical role in promoting diversity. Organizations must proactively seek out and attract diverse talent, ensuring that their recruitment processes are fair, transparent, and free from bias. This may involve expanding recruitment channels, partnering with diverse organizations, and implementing blind resume reviews. It also means ensuring that interview panels are diverse and trained to evaluate candidates objectively, based on their qualifications and potential.

Once hired, employees must be provided with the resources and support they need to thrive. This includes training on unconscious bias, cultural competence, and inclusive communication. It also means creating employee resource groups (ERGs) where employees from underrepresented groups can connect, share experiences, and advocate for their needs. Additionally, mentorship and sponsorship programs can help diverse employees navigate the workplace, build relationships, and access opportunities for advancement.

Building a culture of inclusion requires ongoing effort and attention. Organizations must create safe spaces for open dialogue and encourage employees to share their perspectives and experiences. They must also address microaggressions, which are subtle but harmful comments or behaviors that can make employees from underrepresented groups feel marginalized or excluded. By creating a culture of inclusion, organizations can foster a sense of belonging and empower employees to bring their authentic selves to work.

Promoting diversity and inclusion is not a one-time initiative; it's an ongoing journey. Organizations must continually assess their progress, identify areas for improvement, and adapt their strategies as needed. This may involve collecting and analyzing data on diversity metrics, conducting employee surveys to gauge their experiences, and seeking feedback from diverse stakeholders. By continuously learning and evolving, organizations can create a workplace that truly embraces diversity and inclusion at all levels.

In conclusion, promoting diversity and inclusion is a complex but essential endeavor for any organization that seeks to thrive in the 21st century. It requires a commitment from leadership, intentional recruitment and hiring practices, ongoing training and development, a culture of inclusion, and continuous evaluation and improvement. By embracing diversity and inclusion, organizations can unlock the full potential of their workforce, drive innovation, and create a more equitable and fulfilling workplace for all. Remember, diversity is not just a buzzword; it's a business imperative that can lead to greater success, innovation, and social impact.

ၒၒၒ

Diversity is a strength, not a weakness. Embrace the richness of human differences, foster a culture of inclusion, and create a workplace where everyone feels valued, respected, and empowered to contribute their unique talents.

SIXTEEN

THRIVING IN A CHANGING WORK LANDSCAPE

The modern work landscape is a dynamic and ever-evolving environment, characterized by rapid technological advancements, shifting economic conditions, and evolving workforce demographics. For women seeking to thrive in this changing landscape, it's essential to embrace agility, adaptability, and a growth mindset. This involves not only keeping up with the latest trends and technologies but also developing a deep understanding of the forces shaping the future of work and proactively positioning oneself for success.

One of the most significant shifts in the work landscape is the rise of automation and artificial intelligence (AI). While these technologies have the potential to streamline processes and increase efficiency, they also raise concerns about job displacement and the need for upskilling and reskilling. To thrive in this environment, women must embrace lifelong learning, continuously updating their skills and knowledge to remain relevant and competitive. This may involve pursuing additional certifications, attending workshops and conferences, or even exploring entirely new career paths.

The gig economy is another major trend shaping the work landscape. Increasingly, workers are opting for freelance, contract, or project-based work over traditional full-time employment. This shift offers flexibility and autonomy but also requires a different set of skills and strategies. To succeed in the gig economy, women must build a strong personal brand, cultivate a diverse network of clients and collaborators, and develop effective time management and self-marketing skills.

Remote work has become the norm for many professionals, accelerated by the global pandemic. While remote work offers numerous benefits, such as flexibility and reduced commuting time, it also presents unique challenges, such as isolation, communication barriers, and the blurring of boundaries between work and personal life. To thrive in a remote work environment, women must establish clear boundaries, create a dedicated workspace, prioritize communication and collaboration, and proactively seek opportunities for social interaction and connection.

Diversity and inclusion are increasingly recognized as essential for organizational success. Companies are actively seeking to build diverse teams that reflect the communities they serve and bring a wider range of perspectives and experiences to the table. For women, this presents an opportunity to leverage their unique strengths and perspectives to drive innovation, solve complex problems, and make a meaningful impact. By embracing diversity and championing inclusion, women can create a more equitable and fulfilling workplace for all.

The changing work landscape also demands a greater emphasis on soft skills, such as communication, collaboration, problem-solving, and adaptability. These skills are becoming increasingly important as automation takes over routine tasks, leaving humans to focus on more complex and creative endeavors. Women who possess strong soft skills are well-positioned to thrive in this new environment, as they can effectively navigate interpersonal relationships, collaborate with diverse teams, and adapt to changing circumstances.

Thriving in a changing work landscape also requires a proactive approach to career management. This involves setting clear goals, regularly assessing your skills and knowledge, seeking out mentorship and sponsorship opportunities, and building a strong personal brand. It also means being open to new opportunities, embracing change, and continuously learning and growing.

In conclusion, the changing work landscape presents both challenges and opportunities for women. By embracing agility, adaptability, and a growth mindset, women can navigate these changes with confidence and position themselves for success. This involves staying ahead of the curve by continuously learning and upskilling, embracing new work models such as remote work and the gig economy, championing diversity and inclusion, developing strong soft skills, and taking a proactive approach to career management. By embracing the future of work, women can not only survive but thrive in this dynamic and ever-evolving landscape. Remember, the only constant is change, and those who embrace it will be the ones who lead the way in the workplace of tomorrow.

Stress is a part of life, but it doesn't have to control you. Develop healthy coping mechanisms, manage your time effectively, prioritize self-care, and create a healthy work-life balance.

SEVENTEEN
MANAGING WORKPLACE STRESS

Workplace stress is an omnipresent reality in the modern professional landscape. The demands of deadlines, performance expectations, interpersonal relationships, and the constant need to adapt to change can take a toll on even the most resilient individuals. For women, who often juggle multiple roles and responsibilities, managing workplace stress is essential for maintaining well-being, productivity, and overall career success.

Recognizing the signs of stress is the first step towards effective management. Stress manifests differently in different individuals, but common symptoms include irritability, difficulty concentrating, sleep disturbances, changes in appetite, fatigue, and physical ailments like headaches or stomachaches. It's crucial to pay attention to these signals and address them promptly before they escalate into more serious health issues.

Developing healthy coping mechanisms is key to managing workplace stress. This might involve regular exercise, which releases endorphins and reduces stress hormones. Mindfulness practices, such as meditation or yoga, can help calm the mind, reduce anxiety, and improve focus. Spending time in nature has been shown to have a restorative effect on both mental and physical well-being. Adequate sleep, a balanced diet, and staying hydrated are also essential for maintaining energy levels and managing stress.

Time management plays a crucial role in reducing workplace stress. Prioritize tasks, delegate responsibilities, and avoid overcommitting. Set realistic deadlines and break down large projects into smaller, more manageable tasks. Learn to say no to additional commitments that don't align with your priorities or values. By managing your time effectively, you can avoid feeling overwhelmed and maintain a sense of control over your workload.

Building a strong support network is essential for managing stress. Share your concerns and challenges with trusted colleagues, friends, or family members. Seek their advice, encouragement, and support. Joining a professional network or support group can also provide a safe space to share experiences, gain insights, and connect with others who understand the unique challenges you face.

Creating a healthy work-life balance is crucial for managing stress. Make time for activities that bring you joy and fulfillment outside of work, such as hobbies, spending time with loved ones, or volunteering in your community. Setting boundaries between work and personal life is also essential. This might involve limiting after-hours emails and calls, disconnecting from work-related technology during personal time, and creating dedicated time for relaxation and rejuvenation.

Learning to manage your emotions is another important aspect of stress management. When faced with stressful situations, take a few deep breaths, step back, and assess the situation objectively. Avoid reacting impulsively or making hasty decisions. Instead, take the time to process your emotions, seek support if needed, and develop a plan to address the situation in a calm and rational manner.

Developing healthy communication skills can also help reduce workplace stress. Learn to express your needs and concerns clearly and assertively, without becoming aggressive or confrontational. Actively listen to others, seek to understand their perspectives, and work collaboratively to find solutions. By communicating effectively, you can resolve conflicts, build stronger relationships, and create a more positive and supportive work environment.

Setting realistic expectations is crucial for managing stress. Don't strive for perfection; instead, strive for excellence. Recognize that everyone makes mistakes, and it's okay to not have all the answers. Focus on your progress, celebrate your successes, and learn from your challenges. By setting realistic expectations, you can reduce the pressure you put on yourself and create a more positive and empowering work experience.

Seeking professional help is a sign of strength, not weakness. If you're struggling to manage workplace stress on your own, don't hesitate to seek help from a therapist or counselor. They can provide you with tools and strategies to cope with stress, manage your emotions, and build resilience. They can also help you identify the root causes of your stress and develop a personalized plan for overcoming them.

Remember, managing workplace stress is an ongoing process that requires continuous effort and attention. It's about developing healthy habits, building a supportive network, setting boundaries, managing your time effectively, and seeking help when needed. By prioritizing your well-being and taking proactive steps to manage stress, you can create a more fulfilling and sustainable work life.

ᐅᐅᐅ

Career transitions are opportunities for growth and renewal. Clarify your goals, assess your skills, build a strong network, and embrace change with confidence and optimism.

EIGHTEEN

MAKING CAREER TRANSITIONS WITH CONFIDENCE

Career transitions can be daunting, filled with uncertainty and self-doubt. However, they also present exciting opportunities for growth, renewal, and the pursuit of new passions. For women, making career transitions with confidence requires a strategic approach, self-belief, and a willingness to embrace change. It's about identifying your goals, assessing your skills, building a strong network, and taking bold steps towards a fulfilling and rewarding career path.

The first step in making a successful career transition is to clarify your motivations and goals. Why are you considering a change? What are you hoping to achieve? What are your passions and interests? What skills and experiences do you want to leverage? By understanding your motivations and goals, you can create a clear vision for your future and develop a roadmap for your transition.

Once you've clarified your goals, it's time to assess your skills and experience. What transferable skills do you possess that can be applied to a new field or industry? What additional skills or knowledge do you need to acquire? Take inventory of your strengths, weaknesses, and areas for development. Consider taking online courses, attending workshops or conferences, or seeking mentorship to enhance your skillset and prepare for your transition.

Networking is a crucial component of career transitions. Reach out to your existing network of colleagues, friends, and mentors to inform them of your career goals and seek their advice and support. Attend industry events, conferences, and workshops to meet new people and learn about different career paths. Use online platforms like LinkedIn to connect with professionals in your desired field and learn about job openings.

Building a strong personal brand is essential for a successful career transition. Your personal brand is your unique value proposition, the combination of skills, experience, and personality that sets you apart from others. Develop a clear and compelling brand message that communicates your expertise and passion. Update your resume and online profiles to reflect your new career goals. Be active on social media, sharing your insights and expertise to build your reputation and attract opportunities.

Preparing for interviews is a critical step in the career transition process. Research the company and the position thoroughly. Practice answering common interview questions and prepare thoughtful questions to ask the interviewer. Highlight your transferable skills and experience, and demonstrate your passion and enthusiasm for the new field. Be confident in your abilities and articulate your value proposition clearly and concisely.

Overcoming fear and self-doubt is a common challenge during career transitions. It's natural to feel uncertain and apprehensive about stepping outside of your comfort zone. However, it's important to remember that change is a natural part of life and that growth often occurs outside of our comfort zones. Challenge negative thoughts and replace them with positive affirmations. Focus on your strengths, celebrate your accomplishments, and trust in your ability to succeed.

Embracing change is a key mindset for successful career transitions. The modern workplace is constantly evolving, and the ability to adapt to change is becoming increasingly important. Be open to new ideas, embrace challenges as opportunities for growth, and be willing to step outside of your comfort zone. By embracing change, you can navigate transitions with confidence and resilience.

Remember, making a career transition is a journey, not a destination. It takes time, effort, and a willingness to learn and grow. Be patient with yourself, celebrate your progress, and don't be afraid to ask for help when needed. With a clear vision, a strong network, and a proactive approach, you can confidently navigate your career transition and achieve your professional goals.

ᐅᐅᐅ

Success is a journey, not a destination. Celebrate your wins, big and small, acknowledge your hard work, and share your joy with others.

NINETEEN

CELEBRATING YOUR SUCCESSES

In the relentless pursuit of career mastery, it's easy to get caught in the whirlwind of goals, deadlines, and the constant striving for more. Yet, amidst this pursuit, the importance of celebrating successes often gets overlooked. Recognizing and appreciating your achievements, both big and small, is not merely an act of self-indulgence; it's a crucial element in fostering a positive mindset, maintaining motivation, and fueling your drive for continued growth.

Celebrating success starts with recognizing its many forms. It's not just about the major milestones, like landing a promotion, closing a major deal, or receiving an award. Success can also be found in the everyday victories, the small steps forward, the challenges overcome, and the lessons learned. It's about acknowledging the effort, dedication, and resilience that you put into your work, even when the results may not be immediately apparent.

Celebrating success is not about boasting or seeking external validation. It's about acknowledging your own hard work and appreciating the progress you've made. It's about recognizing the value you bring to your team, your organization, and your community. By celebrating your successes, you reinforce your self-worth, build confidence, and cultivate a positive self-image.

The act of celebration can take many forms. It could be as simple as taking a moment to reflect on your accomplishments, journaling about your wins, or sharing your success with a trusted friend or colleague. It could also involve treating yourself to a special meal, indulging in a hobby, or taking a well-deserved break. The key is to find ways to celebrate that resonate with you and bring you joy.

Celebrating success is not only beneficial for your personal well-being; it also has a positive impact on your professional life. When you celebrate your achievements, you create a positive feedback loop that reinforces your motivation and drive. It reminds you of what you're capable of, fueling your ambition to set new goals and reach even greater heights.

Moreover, celebrating success can inspire and motivate others. When you share your wins with your colleagues, team members, or mentors, you create a positive and supportive work environment. You demonstrate that hard work and dedication are valued and rewarded, and you encourage others to strive for their own goals.

Celebrating success can also be a powerful tool for overcoming setbacks and failures. When faced with challenges or disappointments, it's important to remember your past successes and the resilience you've demonstrated in overcoming obstacles. By celebrating your wins, you remind yourself that you have the strength and capability to overcome any challenge that comes your way.

In the context of career mastery, celebrating success is not just a feel-good activity; it's a strategic tool for personal and professional growth. It helps you stay motivated, focused, and resilient in the face of adversity. It also strengthens your relationships, builds your reputation, and enhances your overall well-being.

So, take the time to celebrate your successes, big and small. Acknowledge your hard work, appreciate your accomplishments, and share your joy with others. By embracing a culture of celebration, you'll not only enrich your own life but also inspire and empower those around you. Remember, success is not just about reaching the finish line; it's about enjoying the journey and celebrating the milestones along the way.

The world needs your unique talents, perspectives, and leadership. Rise above challenges, break barriers, and leave a lasting legacy that inspires and empowers others.

TWENTY

LEAVING A LEGACY OF LEADERSHIP

Leaving a legacy of leadership is not merely about achieving individual success but about inspiring and empowering others to reach their full potential. It's about creating a lasting impact that extends beyond your own career, leaving a mark on your organization, your community, and the lives of those you touch. For women, who have historically faced barriers to leadership roles, leaving a legacy of leadership is a powerful way to pave the way for future generations and create a more equitable and inclusive workplace.

Building a legacy of leadership begins with a commitment to personal and professional growth. Leaders are lifelong learners, constantly seeking new knowledge, skills, and perspectives. They embrace challenges as opportunities for growth, seek feedback from others, and are not afraid to admit their mistakes. By investing in their own development, leaders set an example for others to follow, fostering a culture of continuous learning and improvement.

Effective leadership is rooted in strong values and ethics. Leaders act with integrity, honesty, and transparency. They treat their employees, customers, and partners with respect and fairness. They prioritize the well-being of their teams, create a safe and inclusive work environment, and promote ethical business practices. By embodying these values, leaders build trust and credibility, inspiring others to follow their lead.

Creating a positive and supportive work environment is essential for leaving a legacy of leadership. Leaders foster a culture of collaboration, innovation, and mutual respect. They empower their teams to take ownership of their work, celebrate successes, and learn from failures. They create opportunities for growth and development, providing mentorship and sponsorship to help others reach their full potential.

Developing future leaders is a hallmark of a lasting legacy. Leaders invest time and resources in identifying and nurturing talent within their organizations. They provide opportunities for mentorship, coaching, and leadership development programs. They empower emerging leaders to take on challenging assignments, providing them with the support and guidance they need to succeed. By cultivating the next generation of leaders, they ensure that their legacy lives on long after they are gone.

Giving back to the community is another important aspect of leaving a legacy of leadership. Leaders recognize that their success is not solely their own, but is also due to the support and resources they received from others. They actively seek ways to give back to their communities, whether through volunteering, mentoring, or philanthropic endeavors. By contributing to the greater good, leaders inspire others to do the same, creating a ripple effect of positive impact.

Advocating for change is a powerful way to leave a lasting legacy. Leaders are not afraid to challenge the status quo, speak up against injustice, and advocate for a more equitable and inclusive workplace. They use their influence and platform to champion diversity, equity, and inclusion, ensuring that everyone has a voice and a seat at the table. By advocating for change, leaders pave the way for future generations and create a more just and equitable society.

Building a legacy of leadership is not a solo endeavor. It requires collaboration, teamwork, and the support of others. Leaders recognize that they are part of a larger ecosystem, and they actively seek out partnerships and alliances to achieve their goals. They build strong relationships with their colleagues, mentors, and sponsors, leveraging their collective expertise and influence to create a lasting impact.

Leaving a legacy of leadership is a lifelong journey. It's about continuously learning, growing, and evolving as a leader. It's about staying true to your values, inspiring others to reach their full potential, and creating a positive impact on the world. By embracing these principles, you can leave a legacy that will continue to inspire and empower others long after you are gone. Remember, leadership is not just about what you achieve; it's about who you become and the impact you make on the lives of others.

Your career is a marathon, not a sprint. Pace yourself, prioritize your well-being, and cultivate a sustainable approach that allows you to thrive both personally and professionally.

TWENTY-ONE
SUMMARY

"Rising Above and Rising with Grace: A Woman's Roadmap to Career Mastery" is a comprehensive guide for women navigating the complexities of the professional world. This book delves into the essential skills, strategies, and mindset shifts necessary for women to achieve their full potential and create a lasting legacy of success.

The journey begins with unleashing your inner potential, a process of self-discovery that involves identifying your values, passions, and strengths. It's about recognizing the unique value you bring to the table and cultivating self-belief to overcome limiting beliefs and embrace your authentic self. Continuous learning and growth, along with a supportive environment, are key to unlocking your full potential and creating a fulfilling career path.

Building confidence from within is another crucial aspect of career mastery. It's a journey of self-awareness, self-compassion, and positive self-talk. Setting and achieving goals, stepping outside of your comfort zone, and surrounding yourself with positive and supportive people are essential for building unshakeable confidence that will empower you to pursue your dreams and overcome challenges.

Setting powerful career goals provides a roadmap for success. It involves clarifying your aspirations, translating them into specific, measurable, achievable, relevant, and time-bound (SMART) goals, and creating a plan to achieve them. Flexibility, visualization, accountability, and regular review are essential for staying on track and adapting to the ever-changing professional landscape.

Navigating workplace dynamics requires emotional intelligence, effective communication, and a nuanced understanding of the unwritten rules that govern professional relationships. Building strong relationships with colleagues, supervisors, and stakeholders, resolving conflicts constructively, and understanding office politics are all essential skills for navigating the complexities of the workplace.

Mastering the art of networking is another crucial aspect of career advancement. It's about creating authentic connections, fostering mutual support, and building a community of like-minded professionals who can uplift and empower you. Networking opens doors to new opportunities, provides access to valuable information and resources, and can lead to lifelong friendships and collaborations.

Communicating with impact and influence is a skill that transcends industries, roles, and hierarchies. It involves clarity, storytelling, nonverbal communication, active listening, conciseness, persuasion, adaptability, relationship building, and continuous learning. By mastering these elements, you can transform your communication into a powerful tool for inspiring action, driving change, and achieving your goals.

Developing leadership skills is essential for women who aspire to break barriers and achieve career mastery. It involves inspiring and motivating others, communicating effectively, building strong relationships, making sound decisions, solving problems creatively, adapting to change, demonstrating resilience, and leading with integrity and ethics.

Negotiating for your worth is a critical skill that can significantly impact your career trajectory and financial well-being. It's about advocating for yourself, recognizing your value, and ensuring that you are fairly compensated for your contributions. By researching industry standards, preparing thoroughly, projecting confidence, and being open to dialogue, you can negotiate effectively for your worth and achieve a fair and equitable outcome.

Finding mentorship and sponsorship can provide invaluable guidance, support, and advocacy as you navigate your career journey. Mentors offer advice, share their experiences, and help you navigate challenges, while sponsors actively advocate for your advancement, opening doors to new opportunities. By seeking out and nurturing these relationships, you can accelerate your career growth and achieve your full potential.

Building a strong personal brand is essential for distinguishing yourself in the competitive professional landscape. It involves defining your unique value proposition, crafting a compelling brand message, and consistently embodying your brand through your online presence, content creation, and professional interactions. By building a strong personal brand, you can enhance your credibility, attract opportunities, and achieve greater visibility and recognition.

Achieving a healthy balance between career and personal life is essential for overall well-being and long-term success. It involves redefining what balance means to you, setting boundaries, managing your time effectively, prioritizing self-care, embracing flexibility, communicating openly with your loved ones and colleagues, seeking help when needed, and setting realistic expectations.

By integrating your work and personal life in a way that feels fulfilling and sustainable, you can create a harmonious and rewarding life.

Overcoming imposter syndrome, the pervasive feeling of self-doubt and inadequacy despite external evidence of success, is a common challenge for women in the workplace.

By acknowledging your feelings, challenging negative self-talk, focusing on your achievements, building a strong support network, seeking professional help, reframing your perspective, setting realistic expectations, and celebrating your successes, you can overcome imposter syndrome and unleash your full potential.

Embracing failure as a stepping stone is a transformative mindset that can lead to greater resilience, innovation, and success.

By viewing setbacks as opportunities for growth and learning, you can extract valuable lessons from your experiences, develop resilience, and emerge stronger and wiser from every challenge.

Cultivating resilience and adaptability are essential for navigating the ever-changing work landscape. Resilience is the capacity to withstand and recover from adversity, while adaptability is the ability to adjust to new or changing circumstances.

By developing these qualities, you can embrace change, overcome obstacles, and thrive in a dynamic and uncertain environment.

Promoting diversity and inclusion is a fundamental pillar of a thriving and equitable workplace. It involves creating a culture where everyone feels valued, respected, and empowered to contribute their unique perspectives and talents.

By embracing diversity and inclusion, organizations can unlock the full potential of their workforce, drive innovation, and create a more equitable and fulfilling workplace for all.

Thriving in a changing work landscape requires agility, adaptability, and a growth mindset. It involves keeping up with the latest trends and technologies, embracing new work models, championing diversity and inclusion, developing strong soft skills, and taking a proactive approach to career management.

By embracing change and continuously learning and growing, you can position yourself for success in the workplace of tomorrow.

Managing workplace stress is essential for maintaining well-being, productivity, and overall career success. By recognizing the signs of stress, developing healthy coping mechanisms, managing your time effectively, building a strong support network, creating a healthy work-life balance, learning to manage your emotions, communicating effectively, and seeking professional help when needed, you can reduce stress and create a more positive and productive work environment.

Making career transitions with confidence requires a strategic approach, self-belief, and a willingness to embrace change. It involves clarifying your goals, assessing your skills, building a strong network, preparing for interviews, overcoming fear and self-doubt, embracing change, and seeking support when needed.

By taking a proactive approach and embracing the journey, you can successfully navigate your career transition and achieve your professional goals.

Finally, celebrating your successes is not just an act of self-indulgence but a crucial element in fostering a positive mindset, maintaining motivation, and fueling your drive for continued growth.

By recognizing and appreciating your achievements, both big and small, you can reinforce your self-worth, build confidence, and inspire others to strive for their own goals.

In conclusion, "Rising Above and Rising with Grace" provides a comprehensive roadmap for women seeking career mastery. By embracing these principles, strategies, and mindset shifts, you can unlock your full potential, overcome challenges, and create a fulfilling and impactful career that leaves a lasting legacy of leadership.

ᐁᐁᐁ

Citation And References

This book represents the culmination of extensive research and meticulous analysis, incorporating a diverse range of sources, including numerous books, scholarly studies, and personal experiences. Additionally, I have scoured various websites to gather relevant information and data essential for the compilation of this work. I have taken every precaution to ensure the accuracy of the information presented and have diligently cited all sources to acknowledge their contributions.

Despite these efforts, the possibility of inadvertent errors remains. I deeply value the insights of my readers and appreciate any feedback that can help identify and rectify such inaccuracies. I encourage you to bring any discrepancies to my attention.

Your feedback is not only welcome but crucial, as it will aid in correcting current editions and enhancing the content of future ones. I am committed to maintaining the highest standards of accuracy and reliability in my work and thank you for your support and understanding.

Additionally, I firmly uphold the principle of freedom of speech and expression as guaranteed under Article 19(1)(a) of the Constitution of India, and I respect the diverse viewpoints and expressions of all readers.

ppp

Other Books Of The Author

1. Empowering Minds: A Journey into Women's Self-Discovery and Power
2. The Dynamics of Motivation: Catalyzing Thought into Action
3. Meditation and Mental Well Being: The Path to Inner Peace and Clarity
4. The Psychology of Child Education: Nurturing Future Generations
5. Ethical Enlightenment: A Modern Guide to Living with Integrity
6. Voices of Empowerment: Stories of Women Rising Against Odds
7. Social Psychology in Everyday Life: Understanding Human Connections
8. The Essence of Motivational Speaking: Inspiring Change in Others
9. Balancing Acts: Women, Work, and the Will to Lead
10. Guiding with Grace: Raising Children with Compassion and Awareness
11. The Power of Positive Aging: Embracing Life After Fifty
12. Building Resilient Communities: Social Work in Action
13. The Ethical Educator: Principles for Teaching and Learning
14. From Insight to Impact: Social Psychology for a Better World
15. The Ethics of Empathy: A Guide to Ethical Living
16. The Science of Empowering the Self: Navigating Life's Challenges with Psychological Wisdom
17. The Mindful Conscious Leader: Meditation Techniques for Modern Management
18. Pioneering Spirit: Women's Pathways to Leadership and Empowerment
19. Feeling to Healing: The Role of Emotional Intelligence in Child Development
20. Transformative Talks and Words of Inspiration: Insights into Motivational Oratory

21. Green Ethics: A Path to Sustainable Living
22. Spiritual Integrity: Navigating Life with Moral Compassion
23. Clean Living, Clean Society: The Ethics of Cleanliness
24. Patriotic Spirits: Building a Nation on Positive Attitudes
25. Innovative Integrity & Vibrant Visions: The Ethical and Entrepreneurial Spirit of Gujarat
26. Youthful Visions, Endless Possibilities: Inspiring Ethics and Motivation in Children
27. Living Your Legacy: How to Motivate Others by Living Your Values
28. Secret of Healing Conversations: Ethical Practices in Counselling and Therapy
29. Creative Kindness: Crafting a Life of Compassion and Creativity
30. The Power of Appreciation: How Gratitude Can Transform Your Relationships
31. Bhagavad-Gita: Messages
32. Science of Art: The New Frontier of Fashion Modernism
33. Vivekananda's Virtues: A Blueprint for Modern Living
34. Empower Her: Navigating the Path to Women's Entrepreneurship
35. The Boundless Classroom: Innovations in Global Education
36. The Language of Leadership: Communicating with Authenticity and Impact
37. The Warrior's Mantra: Deciphering the Hanuman Chalisa
38. Echoes of Empathy: Transformative Stories of Social Service
39. Artful Living: Cultivating Creativity in Your Daily Routine
40. Finding Your Why: Discovering Your Passions and Charting Your Course
41. The Role of Social Media in Shaping Self-Esteem and Interpersonal Relationships among Adolescents
42. Karma's Tapestry: Weaving a Life of Selfless Service
43. Altruistic Alchemy: Transforming Lives Through Giving
44. The Blueprint of Pro-Activeness and Productivity: Crafting Habits for Success
45. The Simplicity with Grounded Wisdom: Embracing Authenticity

72. The Resilience Factor: Transforming Setbacks into Stepping Stones
73. The Healing Touch of Nature: An Introduction to Naturopathy
74. Echoes of the Past: Healing Through Past Life Regression
75. The Spiritual Healer's Handbook: Exploring Energy Medicine
76. Crystal Clarity: Unveiling the Power of Gemstones
77. The Dream Weaver's Guide: Decoding the Language of Dreams
78. Emotional Alchemy: Transforming Pain into Power
79. Sonic Serenity: Harnessing Sound for Stress Relief
80. The Entrepreneur's Playbook: Launching Your Business with Confidence
81. Productivity Unleashed: Time Management Strategies for Entrepreneurs
82. The Problem Solver's Toolkit: Creative Solutions for Business Challenges
83. The Future is Now: Emerging Trends in Business
84. The Curious Explorer: A Child's Guide to Scientific Discovery
85. Digital Pioneers: Empowering Kids in the Tech World
86. The Young Philosopher's Guide: Exploring Life's Big Questions
87. Finding Your Voice: Communication Skills for Confident Kids
88. Nature's Playground: A Child's Guide to Outdoor Adventure
89. Growing a Greener Tomorrow: A Guide to Tree Planting & Conservation
90. Driving with Purpose: Ethical Choices on the Road
91. The Healing Touch: Cultivating Compassion in Healthcare
92. Navigating the Digital Landscape: Ethics in the Age of Social Media
93. The Ethical Closet: A Guide to Sustainable Fashion
94. The Mindful Voyager: Sustainable Travel Practices
95. The Feminine Divine: Honoring the Goddesses of India
96. Sacred Sounds: Chanting Your Way to Inner Peace
97. The Yoga Path: Uniting with the Divine Within
98. Rites of Passage: Creating Meaningful Ceremonies
99. The Chakra System: A Map of Inner Transformation
100. Spiritual Sangha: Finding Community through Satsang and

Bhajan

101. Pilgrimage of the Soul: Spiritual Journeys in India

❧❧❧

Contact

Dr. Minakshi Bansal
Social Activist
Ahmedabad, Gujarat, Bharat
minakshiindiag20@yahoo.com

❧❧❧

|| LOKAHA SAMASTHAHA SUKHINO BHAVANTU ||